ANGER AND FORGIVENESS

ANGER AND FORGIVENESS

Raymond Lloyd Richmond, Ph.D.

radeMark
PUBLISHING
CINCINNATI, OHIO

Cover by Kathy Holbrook

Published in the United States by
Trademark Publishing, Cincinnati, OH

ISBN-10: 0-9786627-0-9
ISBN-13: 978-0-9786627-0-7
Library of Congress Control Number: 2006905396

Revised Third Printing July 2006
Printed in the United States of America

CONTENTS

Part One

ANGER

Man's anger does not fulfill God's justice. If a man who does not control his tongue imagines that he is devout, he is self-deceived; his worship is pointless.

JAMES 1:20, 26

1   APATHY

It began with a simple drive to the airport. But, before long, she began to criticize his driving: he wasn't aggressive enough; he wasn't pushing far enough past the speed limit; they would be late and it would be his fault. He, though, ever patient and peaceful, took it all silently.

They were hardly speaking by the time they arrived at the airport.

Then something strange happened.

She got out of the car in a huff and walked away. He just sat there, watching her. And he felt nothing. He had no urge to run after her. He didn't care whether he ever saw her again or not.

Later, when he remembered this incident in psychotherapy for his depression, he broke into tears. His apathy that day shocked him. When I suggested that he might have been angry with her, he protested, "But I love her. How can I be angry with her?"

Poor guy. Little did he understand love. And little did he understand anger.

2 ANGER

Let's face it—anger is a fact of life. Our world is filled with hatred, aggression, and violence. Psychologically, many theories of human development focus on the infant's struggle with anger and frustration and the primitive fantasies of aggression, guilt, and reparation that result from these feelings. In essence, we grow up with anger right from the beginning of life.

> The brilliant French psychoanalyst, Jacques Lacan, taught that aggression occurs as a psychological defense against threats of *fragmentation*. [1]

> That is, as infants, we are just a jumble of diverse biological processes over which we have little or no authority, and our first task in life is to develop a coherent identity that "pulls together" this fragmented confusion. This identity may give the appearance of a unified personality, but it really is just a psychological illusion that hides our essential

> human vulnerability and weakness. And so, when
> anything or anyone threatens us with the truth of
> our essential fragmentation, the quickest, easiest,
> and most common defense available—to hide the
> truth of our weakness and to give the illusion that
> we possess some sort of power—is aggression.

As a result, some persons will fly into a rage about almost anything. But some persons, like the man in the story above, don't get any closer to anger than apathy. And yet apathy really is a veiled form of anger because, like all anger—as will be explained in the pages that follow—apathy, even though it achieves its goal through passive indifference, ultimately wishes harm on another person.

So, given that anger is a human reality, what help can psychology offer in learning to cope with it?

3   THE STARTING POINT:
    THREE STEPS

Even though this might seem like an obviously simple point, many persons still have a deep reluctance to grasp it: *anger is a common human emotion.* We all feel it. And we feel it far more often than we would like to admit.

But before going any further, we need to make a clear distinction between *anger* and *feeling hurt or irritated.*

We all feel hurt or irritated when someone or something obstructs our needs or desires. Anger, though, in its technical sense refers to the desire to "get even with"—that is, to take revenge on—the *cause* of the hurt.

For example, when another car suddenly cuts in front of your car on the road, adrenaline pumps into your bloodstream. Your heart rate jumps. Your blood pressure surges. These things, however, are just immediate fight-or-flight *physiological responses* to any perceived threat.

But then, as a *psychological reaction* to these immediate physical responses, indignation and animosity toward the other driver overrun your mind. You honk your horn. You give a dirty look. You scream a curse. And there you have it: anger. Anger, therefore, is the wish for harm or bad or evil to come upon someone who—in your eyes—has injured you.

So the psychological process is clear and simple. If a person hurts you, then, in your anger, you want to hurt him back, just as you have been hurt.

> Anger can also be expressed indirectly. If something like a traffic jam, for example, leaves you feeling tense and frustrated, then what do you do? Maybe you go home and find some petty thing out of order and then blow up, just to take out your frustration on your family. Or maybe you go to a bar, maneuver someone into offending you, and get into a fight. Either way you vent your frustrations at the traffic jam by hurting innocent persons—after first unconsciously manipulating circumstances so that you can believe in your own mind that these persons have somehow hurt you and deserve to suffer for it.

Still, there is more to the story than this, because there is more to anger than meets the eye.

The truth is, anger may be a "natural"—that is, a commonly occurring—social reaction to hurt and insult, but being natural doesn't necessarily make it good for us. Sure, "natural" foods are commonly advertised as being healthy and good for us. But poisons, for example, are also natural, and poisons, by definition, are deadly.

And so there are far better ways to cope with hurt and insult than with anger, because anger itself acts like a poison in your own heart that ultimately degrades the quality of your own life as much as it hurts the life of another person.

So the FIRST STEP in learning a healthy response to feelings of hurt and insult is simply to acknowledge that you're hurt.

This is not as easy as it sounds.

For example, when you get angry you don't really allow yourself to feel your inner vulnerability and hurt. All you can think about in the moment is your desire to get revenge. In essence, your outbursts of rage paradoxically hide your inner feelings of vulnerability, so you never *recognize* the hurt you're *feeling* that triggers your hostile reaction. All the bitterness and hostility is a big puff of smoke, an emotional fraud. It hardens your heart toward others so that you can seal off your own emotional pain.

> Years ago I became a very good marksman with a pistol. As I was learning to shoot, I would be told things like, "You're flinching your wrist just before you pull the trigger." But did this stop me from flinching my wrist? No, of course not, because at the beginning I didn't have the experience to discern the subtle muscle actions in my wrist. How could I learn *not* to do something unless I had learned how it felt to *do* it? So, in order to shoot well, I had to train myself to feel the various tiny muscles of my hand and arm; once I felt them, I could then direct them.

> Well, that was all many years ago, and I no longer have much use for guns, but I learned a good psychological lesson from it. How can you learn *not* to do something unless you understand quite clearly how it *does* feel to do it? How can you learn *not* to respond defensively to a feeling of vulnerability unless you understand quite clearly how it *does* feel to be vulnerable? If you are always hiding your hurt feelings behind a protective show of bitter curses (or weapons) you will never catch on to the concept

of enlightened emotional restraint simply because
you won't allow yourself to *feel* what must be re-
strained.

Or you might feel hurt by someone emotionally close to
you, and, because you fear that your immediate impulse
to hurt that person will cause you to lose that person's
"love," you suppress the awareness of your inner feelings.
If you do this often enough you can end up convinc-
ing yourself that everything is fine and peaceful. In this
case the hurt becomes anger anyway, only it becomes
unconscious anger: you remain hurt while the desire to
hurt the other person gets pushed into your unconscious where it stews in bitter resentment. Therefore, in
reality, you are just deceiving yourself and defiling your
relationships when you *deny* that you have anything to
feel hurt about. And, before you know it, right in the
middle of all this self-deception, you will be wondering
why you're so depressed. Depression, after all, is often
"anger turned inwards"— that is, you end up despising
yourself because you feel guilty for unconsciously wanting to hurt someone else.

In Western psychology, acceptance of every person's unique emotional experiences is common-
place, but many non-Western cultures place a high
value on social conformity. As a way to ensure a
child's survival in such a culture, families teach chil-

dren that all expressions of anger are forbidden and shameful. And to accomplish this, parents, along with the rest of society in general, tend to suppress all recognition of individual emotions.

Hurt feelings in response to injury or insult, however, are universally human. If these feelings are suppressed in any culture to the point that they never become recognized or named, they can fuel the ugly cultural shadows of prejudice, hatred, paranoia, child abuse, domestic violence, drug addictions—and all other dark psychological poisons that defile real love—as well as depression itself, which, sadly, can also feel shameful.

It's ironic, then, that a healthy response to feelings of hurt and insult actually leads to compassion and peace, while the suppression of emotions, in trying to protect the surface peace, only leads to a psychological undercurrent of suspicion and cruelty. That's why people who become social "doormats" and let others walk all over them, rather than admit that they feel hurt about anything, usually have quite a lot of resentment and "dirt" underneath their appearance of welcome.

So the SECOND STEP in learning a healthy response to feelings of hurt and insult is to follow the hurt back into its roots in the past to all those times

and circumstances when you felt the same way.

You need to do this because any insult in the present is magnified by similar insults from the past. Failure to recognize old insults only makes the current insult seem far larger than it really is.

> This entire process is a bit like what happens when an insect stings you and you feel a pain way out of proportion to the size of the stinger. First you simply recognize that it hurts. Then you have to explore the wound to find the stinger. The stinger represents the insult that hurts you, digging out the stinger represents the psychological task of realizing how this one insult pierces deep into your self-esteem, and the venom which spreads into the surrounding tissues represents the way unconscious resentment about all sorts of old emotional injuries from the past continues to poison you even in the present.

Having acknowledged the wound and explored it, you will be ready for the healing process to begin. But, for healing to take place, you must be careful to avoid anything that irritates, rather than soothes, the wound.

Therefore, the THIRD STEP in learning a healthy response to feelings of hurt and insult is to avoid the popular response to feelings of hurt and insult.

So let's move on to discover just what this popular response to feelings of hurt and insult might be.

4 THE POPULAR RESPONSE: REVENGE AND VIOLENCE

W hy do we have such a hard time recognizing our feelings of vulnerability and hurt when we are insulted?

Well, go back to that image of that car cutting in front of you. Your heart will be pounding, but, if you are like most persons, you won't be consciously aware of it. Your first conscious reaction will probably be to mutter—or yell—a curse.

But then what?

Well, it all sinks down into the unconscious where fantasies (that is, fleeting mental images, often only subliminally perceived) wage their private wars of revenge.

> I once had to sit through a Rambo movie with some family members. There he was with those half-asleep Italian eyes, his muscles twitching, silently

> taking the insults. "Oh, oh!" they said. "He's get-
> ting angry. Don't make Rambo get angry!" they all
> gloated. And then they were slapping themselves
> and cheering as he hefted his huge machine gun
> and opened fire.
>
> And this is what our culture teaches us—through
> ready-made fantasies in movies, television, music,
> popular literature, and advertising, and acted out
> in politics, sports, and even in our legal system—
> about responding to insult.

Revenge permeates our culture because it permeates the human unconscious. Revenge, therefore, is what we most commonly experience in our unconscious fantasies when we become frustrated.

It could be the intellectual frustration of knowing that others are missing the point. It could be the social irritation of having to tolerate rude behavior. It could be the humiliating insult of not having our expectations fulfilled. It could be the traumatic insult of childhood physical, emotional, or sexual abuse. But insult it is, and as a consequence we will feel the *urge* to pick up weapons—whether physical (i.e., guns and bombs) or verbal (i.e., sarcasm and curses)—and turn them on others.

Often, these urges to get revenge break out of the unconscious into the real world and become real aggression such as terrorism, school violence, or suicide.

Or, in our deepest hurt and frustration, we will turn those weapons on ourselves as a form of self-sabotage. This self-sabotage brings with it the unconscious satisfaction of inflicting guilt on those around us—that is, we secretly hope that our self-inflicted suffering will "say" to others, "Look what *you* made me do to myself!" In this case, our frustrations can stay within us as silent guilt-inducing fantasies lurking behind our social injuries.

Therefore, regardless of whether it's expressed as overt social aggression or silent self-sabotage, the "popular" response to insult is revenge. Thus all anger is, at its core, a dark and cruel wish for harm to come upon the person who hurt you.

This explains why there is so much actual violence in the world. Despite our common sentimental claims about the value of peace, our culture teaches us *by daily example* that insult merits immediate revenge.

Thus, many persons blindly follow the path of violence—and in so doing, they "get angry" to avoid *feeling* the hurt that holds the acknowledgment of their own vulnerability.

This also explains why many persons are so afraid to acknowledge any awareness of their own anger. They have a good sense of where their unconscious wants to take them, and they can't bear the thought of "killing" someone close to them when they feel hurt. So they will stifle everything, right from the beginning; the hurt leads to anger, all right, but they just deny they feel anything, and so they drive the anger deep into the unconscious. They present themselves to the world as calm and level-headed persons who would never even hurt a fly.

> Have you ever seen a child, hurt by something said or done to her, blurt out, "I hate you! I wish you were dead!" and then run to her room and throw herself, sobbing, on her bed?

> When the tears dry, nothing is ever said again about the words of her outburst. Maybe her mother or father will come in and comfort her, or maybe her sister or brother will just start playing with her again, but those words—"I hate you, I wish you were dead"—just get swept off into some dark corner of forgotten memories to collect cobwebs of guilt.

> Well, this is the sort of thing I'm talking about when I mention wanting to "kill" someone. It's a very subtle thing—not the plot of an egregious crime. It's the confused experience of childlike hurt and anger.

So remember that just as wanting to "kill" someone is not necessarily a desire to commit an actual crime, a fantasy of revenge is not necessarily a desire to inflict actual hostility. Sometimes it is just a silent mental wish to see someone get paid back, a wish to feel the satisfaction of knowing that the one who causes hurt will get hurt in the end. And sometimes revenge is just a desire to keep your mouth shut when you might be able to redress a wrong. Again, it's all very subtle with roots deep in childhood insecurity.

> In fact, the proof of all this can be found in Obsessive-Compulsive Disorder where a person who feels overwhelmingly ashamed of these fantasies of revenge will unconsciously construct elaborate rituals to neutralize—or undo—these "bad" thoughts.

> It's similar to Lady Macbeth, in Shakespeare's play *Macbeth*, crying, "Out, damned spot!" as she tries compulsively to rub the stain of Duncan's murder from her hands. [2]

5   THE SOLUTION:
THE FOURTH STEP

So we all suffer insult, and we all feel hurt, and we all tend to sink into fantasies of revenge. Some of us then "get angry" and violently act out the fantasies in real life. And some of us just push everything out of awareness and pretend we are "nice" persons. Is there any honest alternative?

Well, you can get up the courage to explore the human psyche a bit more deeply than most persons want to go and discover something about human nature. Something ugly.

You will discover a concept about human psychology that theology and religion have for ages called *sin*. I won't offer a theological definition of sin here, but a secular, philosophical understanding of the concept could describe it as a sort of *infatuation with the vanity of your personal desires and a reliance on social prestige or power to defeat anyone who stands in the way of your getting what you want.* Or, to say it more simply, most people are narcissistically preoccupied with their immediate desires and have little, if any, altruistic awareness of anyone else around them. Psychologically, this behavior allows you to "feel good" about yourself while stepping on someone else. Based in a fear of love, this behavior leads you away from true love and compassion, and it sends you right into all the predicaments of self-indulgence.

> Now, there is in clinical psychology the diagnosis called *Narcissistic Personality Disorder* which refers to a pervasive pattern of grandiosity (in fantasy or behavior), a need for admiration, and a lack of empathy.
>
> But, in its more universal sense, *narcissism* can be found at the core of almost all psychological dysfunction, for it represents the way we all, like the Greek god Narcissus himself, can "fall in love" with ourselves to hide our own inadequacy and consequently treat others like objects to make ourselves feel strong and competent.

Therefore, if you understand this dark psychological fact about human nature—that everyone is drawn away from essential human goodness by a need to avoid feeling weak or foolish—then you have a new way to cope with your feelings of hurt and to overcome the "natural," hostile slide into anger.

Instead of taking all insults personally, you can realize that every insult derives from that universal tendency in human nature toward selfish, inconsiderate behavior. Given this ugly reality, no cache of guns or bombs or witty insults or curses can be sufficient to eradicate its evil effects from the world, so revenge becomes futile. The only sane response to insult is deep sorrow for all of humanity and compassion for every misguided person who gets caught up in the "popular" way of behaving.

Therefore, the FOURTH STEP in learning a healthy response to feelings of hurt and insult is forgiveness.

To forgive someone means that you consciously make the decision to set aside any desire to see that person hurt because of the hurt he or she caused you, and instead you wish that the person will recognize his or her hurtful behavior, feel sorrow for it, and learn eventually to be a more considerate person. Forgiveness, then, means that you desire healing not just for yourself but also for anyone who hurts you.

This, too, like the first step, is not as easy as it sounds.

For the truth of the matter is that *you cannot forgive*

someone until you have fully felt the pain he or she has caused you.

Pushing the pain into your unconscious, as described earlier, only makes forgiveness impossible because, as unconscious anger, the dark wish to harm the person who hurt you remains alive but out of sight. And, with your animosity kept out of sight, it's all too easy to present yourself as a "nice" person when, deep inside, you really remain an angry victim.

> Those who know true love act with confidence, straightforwardness, and honesty, whereas those who present themselves as nice are often merely hiding the depths of their anger behind a show of smiling appeasement.

For example, many persons who, for one reason or another, seek psychotherapy, would likely endorse the statement, "I am a forgiving person." And they will resist any attempt to look at angry feelings toward their parents, for example, saying that such exploration is just "parent bashing."

But psychological healing really has nothing to do with blaming others.

In order to live honestly and take full responsibility for

your own life, you have to learn to put your hurt and anger onto the "table" in front of you so that you can examine your emotions consciously. And then, when your hurt has been brought to the surface and acknowledged, it can be swept away in forgiveness. But, until this work has been done thoroughly, the statement "I am a forgiving person" is just an illusion.

And the illusion is shown for what it is when many unsuspecting persons say, "OK. I've talked about my traumas. I've forgiven everyone. It's all on the table. But I'm still miserable. What's wrong?" It's as if, after having made what seems to be a simple act of forgiveness, they walk past that "table" and say, "What's that odd smell?" And then, as they look more closely and admit all the things they have been hiding from themselves, they find an ugly, moldy mass of *unconscious anger* that has been growing secretly underneath the table. So that, too, has to be examined. And then, when *everything* has been brought to light, real forgiveness can be possible.

> To forgive means simply that you refuse to keep hating someone—which, in practical terms, means that, from the depths of your heart, you must give up your desire to feel the satisfaction of knowing that the one who caused your hurt will get hurt in the end. It's the silent, secret desire for *satisfaction* that keeps unconscious anger alive and growing.

There are also many persons who deny the concept of "sin." In a practical sense, this denial serves as a psychological defense to protect these persons from the recognition of the ugly parts of their own unconscious. Terrified of looking into the darkness of their unconscious, they just refuse to admit that they are capable of inflicting their own harmful wishes on another person.

> Some popular teachings advocate forgiveness while also denying the reality of sin, saying that all insult lies in our own "perceptions" and that in effect we are all totally free of what we did because "nothing really happened." Ironically, the proof of the reality of sin emerges from within these very groups who deny it, for they are torn by internal factions that are not only judgmental of each other but also bitterly refuse to forgive one another. They may not believe in sin, but it is breeding right under their noses.

So beware. There is no escaping the psychological effects of injury and anger; either you can face up to all of your unconscious anger and learn real forgiveness, or you can let the deadly poison of revenge become your ugly destiny.

> It might be asked, "What about national defense? How can forgiveness and the need for self-defense be reconciled?"

Well, I'm not about to try to tinker with national defense strategy, whether through commentary or through protest. We live in a secular world with secular governments that use popular, secular means, such as aggression and revenge, to sustain and protect themselves.

Psychology, however, concerns the individual, and forgiveness is an individual act. And for that matter, peace is also a matter of individual will, not of politics. No government can order you to love, and no government can order you to hate. Ultimately you have to live—and die—with the destiny of your own conscience.

In all of this, there is only one truth: *If you want to change the world, begin by changing yourself.* If you want the world to be more fair, treat the world fairly even when you are treated unfairly. If you want the world to be more kind, treat the world with kindness and return a blessing for every insult. Show the world by your good actions—not by empty protest or with violence—that you are willing to live according to what you profess to believe.

6 VICTIM ANGER

According to the principles of geometry, an infinite number of lines can be drawn through a single point. To define any one particular line, however, two points are needed.

The same sort of principle applies to psychology. The experience of one trauma, for example, does not tell you much about your unconscious, because any explanation is as good as any other. If you are raped once, or if you get in a car crash, no one has a right to point at you and say, "You did this wrong," or "You did that wrong." It's simply impossible to deduce anything psychological from one event.

But if the trauma is repeated, then you have two points to define a line that can be tracked back into the past and projected into the future. This is the time to sit up and take notice, because if you don't, there will likely be a third time. And there may be others again, until you start to look at your life and ask yourself what is going on.

This concept of psychological repetition, however, has nothing to do with naturally recurring cycles. If your neighbor wakes you up early every morning when he goes to work, for example, you might feel angry, but this isn't *victim anger.*

Repetition refers to an unconscious process by which you essentially lead yourself into trouble over and over. For some dark, unknown reason, you so despise yourself that you continually put yourself at physical or psychological risk. And the failure to accept that this unconscious process has you trapped in its clutches leads to victim anger.

As trauma after trauma batters you, you will begin to say, "Why me? This isn't fair!" You will blame anyone who gets in your way. You will feel like an innocent victim being persecuted by the world. You might even become a psychological "terrorist" whose unconscious objective is to undermine the structure of any authority perceived to be unjust and uncaring. But because you can't look at your responsibility in what is happening, you will develop a *victim mentality*, believing that every painful event in your life is "their" fault, and you will have fallen into victim anger.

A careful distinction must be made here in regard to "naturally" repeated child abuse and repetition. When a child is abused, it cannot be claimed that the child has any responsibility for the abuse. Violence is always the responsibility of the perpetrator, and, when violence is repeated, the perpetrator is at fault. This repeated abuse is therefore not a result of the child's unconscious desires.

But there is a psychodynamic process called *Identification with the Aggressor* in which the abused child, in trying to make sense of something essentially senseless, comes to believe that the abuse must somehow be justified, and the child will therefore unconsciously seek to befriend, and even imitate, the abuser. With this dynamic in place, blame and anger toward the abuser becomes turned toward the self, thus beginning the repetition of an unconscious, self-inflicted abuse.

In fact, scientific research has shown that adults who were sexually abused as children tend to have a high risk for sexual assault (e.g., rape) as adults. Moreover, the research shows that adult sexual assault victims who were also abused as children tend to have even lower levels of mental health functioning than those persons who were sexually abused as children but not revictimized as adults. [3]

So what's going on here? Well, the psychological process of developing an unconscious sense of victim anger is largely a matter of misdirected blame. Here's how it works, in common-sense language:

> 1. As a result of abuse, the child experiences painful fear and hatred of the abuser(s).

> 2. But because the child feels essentially powerless to stop the abuse or to convince anyone to help, the child begins to perceive the whole world as "unfair."

> 3. The child blames the world for being unfair, and, at the same time, begins to blame himself or herself for not being "good enough" to put up a successful fight against the world.

> 4. The child learns that blaming the world does not provide any immediate gratification, and that punishing the world is not an easy task, but that blaming the self—and punishing the self—can provide immediate and controlled satisfaction.

> 5. Because this self-destructive behavior is unconsciously directed against the world,

however, and not against the self, the child
cannot realize, let alone accept consciously,
that he or she is now causing most of his or
her own pain.

6. Therefore, the child grows into an adult
who harbors an aching bitterness against
the world for its unpunished abuses, and,
at the same time, at every disappointment
he or she will find some convenient, secret
means of self-sabotage—and will then feel
justified in saying, "Look what they did to
me! It's not fair!"

And what strange satisfaction maintains all this self-
destruction? Well, it's the satisfaction of *unconsciously
hoping to show the world how wrong it is.* Like Hamlet
holding a mirror up to his mother,[4] hoping that she will
see in herself the responsibility she played in the death
of the king, the person trapped in victim anger will hold
up his own destruction as "evidence" that, he hopes, will
condemn the world.

Thus you might hear someone saying, "So what if I get
cancer from smoking? Maybe it will serve them right.
Then they will see how much I had to suffer." And so
this unfortunate life will end, just like *Hamlet,* cluttered
with death and destruction.

Unlike a martyr, though, who lays down his or her life out of pure love, this self-destruction has its deep motivation in bitterness, hatred, and an obstinate rejection of forgiveness.

When confronted by the victim anger of repetition, therefore, your only hope is first to resolve the repetition that traps you. *You can't forgive others if the real problem is yourself.* How can you accept the ugly part of human nature if you can't see it in yourself and if you can't accept your personal responsibility for constantly placing yourself at risk? If you don't recognize the repetition, all the king's horses and all the king's men—and all the anger management classes in the world—won't save you from your own unconscious efforts to destroy yourself as you remain locked in the dark identity of being a victim.

7   SUMMARY

Keep in mind that, when coping with feelings of hurt and insult, anger, being an emotion, is not something you can ever "get rid of." As long as you are alive there will be times when you are insulted and feel hurt. And, as long as there are times when you feel hurt and insulted, you will be pulled down into unconscious fantasies of revenge.

But once you notice that you *feel hurt* you have a choice. You don't have to accept blindly the unconscious slide into revenge.

On the one hand, you don't have to "get angry." That is, you don't have to fly into a rage and scream at others, shout curses, or become abusive or violent. If you tell yourself, "Yes, I hurt. But it is not so much another person hurting me as it is *human nature itself* hurting me, and there's nothing I can do about it, except refuse to return hurt for hurt, sin for sin," then you can feel

33

compassion for the person who hurt you, and you can be forgiving.

> Violence, after all, is nothing more than a fear of love. And when you fear love, where do you turn? You turn to pride—the pride of your own self-defense.

> There's a great secret here that philosophers have known for ages. And it's a secret only because it's so obvious that no one bothers to notice it.

> Consider the nature of water, a weak and lowly substance that flows freely around all obstacles. If you live a life of the same "humility" as water, even the jaws of hell cannot bite into you. But the more solid you become in the pride of your own strength to avenge yourself against insult, the more those jaws have to grasp onto—and once they have you, then you can't fight free, no matter how many bandoliers you have draped over your shoulders.

> So the more you let go of your "identity"—the more you "die" to yourself in perfect humility—the less you have to defend; and the less you have to defend, the less reason you have for anger.

On the other hand, all of this does not preclude the

possibility that there may be times when you have to stand up—to defend yourself or to defend others—and say something about the ugliness that everyone wants to ignore or deny. To be quiet—to stifle your feeling offended—is also a fear of love and a slide into revenge.

In these situations—whether in your family, among friends, or at work—when you experience feelings about anything, you need only express those feelings openly.

> The key to all this, however, is that you speak up as soon as you feel the first inkling of injury—and this means that you have to be very good at recognizing the feeling of hurt in the first place. You must speak up well before the hurt turns to anger and has any chance to build into something destructive.
>
> Just learn to speak your inner experience honestly in the moment. You don't have to understand *why* you are feeling what you're feeling in the moment; just communicate *what* you're feeling.

It should be no surprise, however, that most persons do not like to hear the "truth" about themselves, so a lot of anger can come back at you for being blunt and honest, and you might feel the urge to back down.

In keeping your mouth shut, though, you will be trapped

in the vindictive satisfaction of watching others suffer in their own sins. So, if you resist the pull to shrink back, then you will find freedom. You will discover a part of yourself that you can trust to guide you through disputes without injuring yourself or others—because you will be motivated not with unconscious anger and revenge to defend your identity but with love for the good of others.

> When you do speak up, keep in mind an important psychological-social fact: *You cannot control the behavior of others.*
>
> Therefore, whenever you feel the need to say something, ask yourself what you want to happen as a result. If your answer is anything like, "I want this person to . . ." then you probably have the wrong motive. But if your answer is more like, "I just want to clear my conscience and offer the opportunity to heal this relationship. Whatever this person does thereafter is up to him," then you are probably on the right track.
>
> Lest all of this seem too difficult and threatening, just remember that in really loving families all their good-natured bantering and humor is really a psychologically healthy way to release feelings of slight and injury. Gentle humor—in contrast to biting sar-

casm—can, therefore, work wonders.

So there you have it. Someone insults you, you feel the pain, you speak up if necessary, and you forgive. Still, after all this, you might be feeling some lingering emotional arousal. What do you do then? Well, just let that last bit of hurt melt into deep sorrow for the entire world.

Finally, note that even though you can be forgiving about hurts and insults, this does not *automatically* mean that you will also be reconciled with the person who hurt you. For the two of you to be reconciled, the other person must (a) recognize the very real injury inflicted on you and consequently (b) repent that injury and make reparation to you. (See Chapter 12.)

Thus the religious concept of "praying for your enemies" can be expressed psychologically as simply hoping that the person who has injured you will ultimately recognize his or her destructive behavior and repent it—as opposed to your wishing for that person's destruction and thereby preventing any hope of reconciliation.

> Saint Teresa of Avila once had a vision of hell; the place was so horrifying, she said, that she wouldn't wish it on her worst enemies.[5] Think about that.

8   A CULTURAL NOTE

Throughout the world, various cultures have their own specific terms to describe "unhealthy" responses to anger. Below are some of these culture-bound syndromes as described in the American Psychiatric Association's DSM-IV. [6]

- *amok*, in Malaysia, is precipitated by a perceived slight or insult and refers to a period of brooding followed by an outburst of violent or aggressive behavior. Similar patterns are found in Laos, the Philippines, Polynesia (*cafard* or *cathard*), Papua New Guinea, Puerto Rico (*mal de pelea*), and among the Navajo (*iich'aa*).

- *bilis & colera* (or *muina*), among Latinos, describe syndromes whose underlying cause is considered to be anger or rage. Symptoms can include tension, headache, screaming, trembling, stomach disturbances, and even chronic fatigue.

- *hwa-byung* is a Korean syndrome attributed to a suppression of anger. Its symptoms can include insomnia, fatigue, panic, fear of impending death, indigestion, labored breathing, and generalized aches and pains.

These syndromes illustrate one basic point: no matter what language you speak, unless you also understand the language of forgiveness, anger will likely lead you straight into psychopathology.

9   JUST THE FACTS, PLEASE

Many of the persons who need help with anger management have no interest in the psychodynamics of anger, and they are put off by anything suggestive of philosophy or religion. So, because anger is such a large problem in the world today, here is some advice about anger management, reduced to its most basic simplicity.

- *Venting anger does not work.* Even though it might give some immediate emotional satisfaction, venting anger (in technical language called *catharsis*)—whether by yelling obscenities, making obscene gestures, honking the horn of your car, throwing or breaking things, or screaming insults—really does nothing to dispel anger. More often than not, venting anger actually pumps up your emotional arousal and may even prolong it.[7]

So, as I say above, recognize the feeling of anger, but don't act on it. Instead, do the following.

- *Cool down.* Remember the old, stereotypical advice about counting to ten before saying or doing anything when you first feel hurt? Well, it's still good advice. That's because the first reaction to hurt is purely physiological: you receive a rush of adrenaline to prepare you to take action in real danger. But when the hurt comes from an event that poses only a short-term threat—such as when a car cuts in front of you—or threatens your pride far more than your life and safety, then all that adrenaline surging through your body isn't serving any meaningful purpose.

  If you are prone to violence, then walk away from the provocation as soon as you feel the pressure building.

  In most cases, simply taking a few moments to practice some simple relaxation exercises, such as deep breathing, can allow your sympathetic nervous system's arousal to calm down and dissipate by itself. Deep, slow breathing is an automatic physiological effect of being at peace, so when you deliberately take slow, deep breaths you are indirectly telling your body that all danger has now passed; as a consequence, your sympathetic nervous system will stop pumping adrenaline into your body and so your arousal will cease.

Just be careful not to use this cooling-off period to dwell on negative thoughts or you will make matters even worse. In fact, this leads to the next step.

- *Challenge your negative thoughts.* The way we think has a lot to do with the way we feel, so changing your thoughts from a hateful, negative orientation to a calm, positive orientation becomes essential in managing feelings of hurt and insult.

  NEGATIVE: *"[Expletive!] What a piece of [expletive] junk! Now we're going to be [expletive] late! [Expletive!]"*

  POSITIVE: *"OK. It's a flat tire. There was nothing we could have done to prevent it. Let's forget about being on time and just see about getting the tire changed. One thing at a time."*

Or look for a rational explanation:

IRRATIONAL: *"[Expletive!] What a [expletive] jerk! He knew this was an important [expletive] meeting! So why is he [expletive] late?"*

RATIONAL: *"Maybe there was a traffic accident. Maybe they had a flat tire. Who knows? We'll find out in due time."*

- *Ask yourself what you're really feeling.* Many individuals have such a limited knowledge of their emotional life that they tend to lump all their troubling emotions together into what they perceive as anger. But, if you look closely, you might find that behind the anger are more pertinent feelings, such as disappointment, sadness, fear, and so on.

   See the Appendix of this book for a list of emotions that can help you identify what you are actually experiencing.

- *Flow around the obstacle.* Most persons feel frustrated when someone or something obstructs them in some way. And most persons respond to the feeling of frustration by immediately wanting the satisfaction of forcing the "obstacle" to get out of the way—or, if it can't or won't move, to curse it and insult it.

The healthy response to frustration, however, requires a different psychological attitude than *satisfaction*. When feeling frustrated, sit back, relax, and wait. Say to yourself the following:

"As things develop, I will, through listening patiently to guidance from my unconscious, adapt to changing circumstances and grow and develop with them."

"I may not get what I want when I want it; nevertheless, I trust that all things will work out in their own good time, for my ultimate benefit, as long as I remain calm and peaceful and open to changing circumstances."

"I may not get what I want at all, and yet, in remaining calm and attentive, I may discover something else that I need even more than what I thought I wanted."

- *Look at things from the other person's perspective.* Have you ever casually stepped off the curb to cross a street when a driver turning the corner almost hits you? It can be enough to make you swear and bang on his car, right? Now imagine yourself as a driver, in a new neighborhood, a bit confused, traffic everywhere. You stop at a corner, about to turn right. You look all around, left, right, left again. It looks clear. You start to move. And then—where did he come from?! A pedestrian just stepped right in front of you and you barely saw him!

So, think about it now. Which person is in the "wrong"—the driver of the car or the pedestrian? Hmm . . . maybe both? It depends on whether you're in the car or out of it, doesn't it?

And that's the point about perspective. Although some persons are truly selfish and inconsiderate, sometimes a person may simply be distracted or confused, not maliciously trying to get in your way and obstruct you. Looking at the "other side" is called *empathy*, and it can go a long way to calming yourself down, keeping the peace, and fostering an atmosphere of simple courtesy.

By the way, when persons have difficulty understanding emotions and therefore lack the capacity for empathy, it's called *alexithymia*.

- *Ask questions*—that is, when the situation involves someone you know and with whom you have a continuing relationship. Once you understand how to do it, it can be relatively simple to forgive a stranger because you don't even have to say anything. But you have an added responsibility when someone you know hurts you. You must ask questions that get to the psychological cause of the problem; if you don't ask, then the hurt will keep repeating itself, and before long you will become seriously depressed.

  Avoid accusatory questions ("So, you're late again! You're seeing someone else, aren't you?"). Questions such as this only make the other person defensive and resistant. Instead, ask open-ended questions that

gmental questions that bring out true feelings. Here are a few examples:

"What's bothering you?"
"What do you need?"
"What are you disappointed about?"
"What are you worried about?"
"How can I help?"

- **Consider the alternatives.** Well, besides the
  alternative of prison, with its loss of freedom, there is only one other alternative to
  managing feelings of hurt and insult in a
  healthy manner: physical or psychological
  illness. Current medical research—as well
  as traditional psychoanalytic theory—understand that chronic hostility and anger,
  whether unrecognized, suppressed, or vent-
  ed in steaming rage, can be causative fac-
  tors in asthma, autoimmune dysfunction,
  coronary artery disease, cysts, depression,
  headaches, heart attacks, high blood pressure, insomnia, intestinal disorders, lower
  back pain, obsessive-compulsive disorder,
  paranoia, sexual dysfunction, and ulcers.

10   A FINAL SUGGESTION

Perhaps you might want to think of anger as just a lot of hot air. So here's a way to remember how to get some cool AIR.

A   *Adrenaline.*
That initial "rush" in response to an insult is adrenaline. Nothing but adrenaline.

I   *Identify.*
Identify *what* is really happening, *how much* of a threat it really is, and *why* it is happening.

R   *Reaction choice.*
Choose a reaction that is both compassionate and fair, rather than fall headlong into hostility and revenge.

Part Two

FORGIVENESS

But if you do not forgive others, neither will your Father forgive your transgressions.

MATTHEW 6:15

11   FORGIVENESS AND HEALING

Anyone who has ever been victimized—and that includes victims of crime, accident victims, adult survivors of childhood abuse, political prisoners, and so on—must decide whether or not to forgive the perpetrator. There can be no middle ground to this decision: either you decide to forgive the person who hurt you, or you hold on to bitterness and anger.

Holding on to bitterness and anger can cause psychological problems of their own, so if you have ever been victimized, being able to forgive your victimizer will be a crucial part of your healing.

> I've seen individuals, for example, who have lost a family member because of a crime.
>
> The survivors' anger and desire for revenge poison their entire beings. They so focus on what they have lost, and what they wanted the dead person to *be,*

and *do,* for *them,* that they completely miss the opportunity they've been given to learn about real love.

Instead, they seem to believe that hatred, even to the point of capital punishment, will satisfy their thirst for vengeance and will somehow bring them healing. So, with hardened hearts and stiff lips, they say, "I'll never forgive." And the sad thing is that in wishing to send someone to hell they end up sending themselves there as well.

Forgiveness, however, can be a problem for many people simply because they are not clear about what forgiveness really is. All too often we confuse forgiveness with reconciliation, a larger process of which forgiveness is but one part.

12 RECONCILIATION

If one person is injured by another, we could say that the two persons are "pushed apart" by the injury, and so, if they are to become friendly again, this gap between them must be repaired—they must be reconciled. *Reconciliation* comes from the Latin words *re-*, meaning "again," and *conciliare*, which means "to bring together," so reconciliation means "to bring together—or to make friendly—again."

The act of reconciliation involves two parts: forgiveness and penance. Since the present discussion is about understanding forgiveness, let's go on then to define penance.

13 PENANCE: CONFESSION, REPENTANCE, AND PENALTY

Let's imagine that some children are playing a game when someone hits a ball all the way across the street, and the ball smashes through Mrs. Smith's living room window.

It seemed like a small explosion, followed by the shrill clinking of bit upon bit of broken glass. Then silence. Her immediate response was a dull shock, void of emotion. Then her conscious mind began to function again. "What was that?" She felt her heart racing. Fear began to grow. She looked into the living room, and her heart sank at the overwhelming mess on the carpet. Feelings of sadness and astonishment mixed with fear and threat in her mind. A primal concern for her life welled up in her. "Is this the end of the world?" Things remained quiet. Her eyes moved to the fragmented window. "Is someone trying to kill me?" She stared at the mess. A

feeling of rage spoke from deep within her wound-
ed heart: "Who could have done this to me?"

The children do not run away. They go over to Mrs.
Smith's house and knock on the door.

She hears a knock on the door. Adrenaline surges
again; her mind struggles to determine the nature
of the threat. She hears the whispering voices of
children. Suspicious and afraid, she opens the door
cautiously.

The children say, "We're sorry, Mrs. Smith. We were
playing and we broke your window."

"So that's it," she sighs. She feels relief as the explanation comes clear. Then her heart sinks again at
the damage, the mess, and the loss. For an instant,
she wonders what might have happened to her if
she had been in the room at the time the window
shattered. She feels the indignation, and with it she
feels the dull urge to throw the hurt back in their
faces. She makes a hard decision.

Mrs. Smith looks at them and says, "I understand, children. I know you didn't mean to hurt me. But you gave
me a scare for my life. And the window is still broken—
you will have to pay for it." (Let's set aside the concept

of homeowner's insurance for a moment, because this is a story about penance.)

The children say, "OK." They pool together their money, and they give the money to Mrs. Smith so she can repair the window. (Let's set aside the question about whether the children can gather together that much money in the first place. Maybe they have to borrow the money from their parents and agree to pay it back. In any event, they pay Mrs. Smith.)

Now, in this story, there are actually three elements that compose the act of penance.

First is the act of *confession*: admitting the act, as when the children say, "We broke your window." The act has to be admitted, aloud, to the person offended, or the entire process stops and no one gets anywhere.

Second is the act of *repentance*: asking for forgiveness, as when the children say, "We're sorry." Remember, if the children had run away, they would have avoided their responsibility to repair the damage they caused, and so they would have prevented the process of penance from getting started.

And third is the act of *penalty*: accepting the punishment, as when the children say, "OK." After all, a broken window is a broken window, and it has to be fixed. If the children do not pay to fix it, their confession and repentance are really worthless.

(For those of you still thinking about the issue of home-owner's insurance, let's say that Mrs. Smith's insurance pays the damages and the children help Mrs. Smith clean up the mess in her living room. In this case their work would serve to fulfill the function of the penalty.)

> This concept of *penalty* opens up many complicated issues about the legal responsibility of the victimizer to the victim.
>
> For example, if a crime is committed, then criminal law should see to it that the victimizer receives a fair trial and just punishment. As for restitution, either the victimizer personally, or the victimizer's insurance company should pay, willingly and fairly, for damages to the victim's property or health.
>
> Now, these aspects of criminal law should be unambiguous and without any psychological implications.
>
> But it's in the area of civil law that psychological ambiguity arises. If you sue because of a *tort*—that is, a wrongful act or injury—then vengeance can

easily be confused with justice. If you are injured to such an extent or in such a way that is not compensated freely by the victimizer, then a tort case may be justified. But if, for example, you trip over a crack in a sidewalk and sue the city for millions of dollars, then you have crossed over from being victimized into "victim anger," and you have entered the dark psychology of greed and revenge.

All of this points to two facts about the psychology of forgiveness: if you cannot let go of your desire for vengeance, you will never find true healing, and you can never be truly healed if you try to force someone else to pay the cost of your healing.

14 THE PSYCHOLOGY OF FORGIVENESS

In the story above, forgiveness comes when Mrs. Smith says, "I understand." In saying this she indicates that she does not intend to carry a grudge against the children.

So that's the process of forgiveness and reconciliation. The injurious act happens, the children confess and make penance, Mrs. Smith forgives them, and, because of the combination of the penance of the children and the forgiveness by Mrs. Smith, the children and Mrs. Smith are reconciled. It's a nice story.

But what does this mean psychologically?

And what would have happened if the children had run away?

Well, now that you know how forgiveness and penance

work together to make for reconciliation, you can understand that forgiveness is possible even without penance. So even though someone hurts you and refuses to apologize—even if they run away—and even if this means that the relationship cannot be repaired, you can still offer forgiveness for the sake of your own mental health.

That is, forgiveness by itself is still psychologically preferable to holding a grudge, because the bitterness of a grudge works like a mental poison that doesn't hurt anyone but you. Seeking revenge or wishing harm to another person will, at the very minimum, deplete your emotional strength and prevent your wounds from healing. In the worst case, the cold hunger for revenge will make you into a victimizer yourself. Lacking forgiveness, you and your victimizer will be locked together in the hell of eternal revenge.

> In Canto XXXIII of the *Inferno,* the first book of Dante's *Divine Comedy,* Dante tells the story of Count Ugolino della Gherardesca and the Archbishop Ruggieri degli Ubaldini. The two men had been allied by political scheming in 13th century Pisa, but ultimately the Archbishop betrayed Ugolino. The Archbishop arrested Ugolino and sealed the Count—and his sons and grandsons—into a tower to be starved to death. During his poetic pilgrimage

through hell, Dante finds Ugolino and Ruggieri fro-
zen together in one hole, with the Count, who died
consumed with hatred, gnawing upon the Arch-
bishop's skull in his eternal hunger for vengeance.

15   THE PROBLEM OF FAILED
RECONCILIATION

Forgiveness can be very difficult for many individuals simply because they are not clear about what forgiveness really is. All too often forgiveness gets confused with *reconciliation*, a larger process of which forgiveness is but one part, as I said above. And all too often, reconciliation fails. So what does that do to your ability to forgive?

In this world you will likely come across many persons who refuse to make penance for their injurious acts. Hypocritically posing as pillars of their community, they might refuse to confess, to repent, and to accept penalty (like some parents who abuse their children), or they might refuse to repent even though they are forced to pay a penalty (like a sociopathic murderer who sneers at the court as he is sentenced to prison).

You, as the victim, can still forgive anyone, even though,

from what you have read so far, you will know that for-giveness does not involve letting the person "off the hook" legally. Nor does your forgiving someone mean that you *must* be reconciled with that person. Reconcili-ation is made possible only by the free choice of the vic-timizer to repent and to repair the damage of the injury, but forgiveness is always your choice—yours alone.

REMEMBER:
Reconciliation is not possible unless
you are willing to forgive the other person
and
the other person apologizes
and "makes it up" to you.

In our story, even if the children had run away—there-by precluding any reconciliation—Mrs. Smith would still have had the choice of forgiving the children or not. She may have been kind and reflected on times when, as a child, she herself got into trouble accidentally. The children's cowardice would have been a wound between them and her, but it wouldn't have been her doing. Or, refusing to forgive, she may have become bitter, begin-ning a neighborhood feud that went on for generations. Unfortunately, that would have been her doing.

16 A CAUTION ABOUT "PREMATURE" FORGIVENESS

There can, however, be one major psychological complication in regard to forgiveness.

You cannot forgive someone until you have fully felt the pain he or she has caused you.

Imagine the person who says, "I'm at peace with what happened. I'm OK with it. Actually, it doesn't even bother me. But my life is still miserable. What do I do now?"

If you find yourself in this position, in effect saying, "No, it doesn't bother me . . . but I'm still miserable," it is a good psychological clue that there is still something missing.

Usually, this means that you are still unconsciously denying your anger and resentment, so even though you *think* you have come to terms with what happened, there are still emotions about the event that you have pushed out of your conscious awareness. In fact, many persons can get caught up in this *premature forgiveness* as a way to avoid coping with all the unpleasant emotions they would rather not examine.

This can be extremely frustrating because unconscious resentments are essentially *invisible* to logic and reason. Because they represent things you would prefer not to see or feel, they can be discovered only indirectly—such as through troubling dreams or when these unconscious resentments continue to cause discomfort even though it *seems* that everything should be OK.

> You might, for example, resist admitting that you are angry with a person you love. So you unconsciously hide that anger from yourself in a desperate attempt to "protect" your love for that person. Yet in your deception you do nothing but keep your resentments alive, and you effectively defile the very love you want to protect.

> This is a common problem with persons caught up in unconscious anger at their parents. Such persons will try to deny their unpleasant feelings by saying, "But my parents tried their best to be good parents. I have no right to feel irritated with them."

The truth, however, is that even parents who do their best always cause some emotional hurt to their children, even if it's unintentional. And hurt is hurt, regardless of whether it's intentional or unintentional. Even if your best friend steps on your foot accidentally, it still hurts, right?

The therapeutic task, then, is to admit all of your childhood hurt—not to blame your parents, but instead to speak openly about the hurt in order to allow the light of honesty to heal the wounds.

Therefore, as counter-intuitive as it may seem, in having the courage to admit all that anyone has done to hurt you, and in recognizing what you are really feeling, and then in being able to forgive that person—of everything—you will finally discover real love.

All of this shows that the popular advice to "forgive and forget" completely misses the point. *Forgetting*, in technical psychological language, is called *repression*. Whenever something is repressed it just lingers in the dark shadows of the unconscious, along with all the emotions associated with it. And as long as those emotions, especially anger, are brewing secretly in the depths of the unconscious, genuine forgiveness remains impossible.

Therefore, in a case involving unconscious emotions, you might want to consider getting professional psychological help.

17 REPAIRING THE DAMAGE

The story about Mrs. Smith and the children is, in many ways, overly simplified so as to illustrate the basic meaning of confession, penance, and reconciliation as they relate to forgiveness.

Still, the story is not that much different from what would happen if, for example, someone were to back into your parked car and then drive away without leaving his or her name and insurance information in a note. When you discover the damage, you're left feeling violated and helpless. But no amount of swearing will fix anything. Even if your insurance covers the entire cost of the repair, you still have to take your own time and expend your own energy to have the damage repaired. And if you go about the work with bitterness in your heart, the task becomes even more painful and irritating. Holding a grudge against human inconsiderateness hurts only you and makes repairing the damage even more difficult.

Consider also the case of a natural disaster. Your home is damaged or destroyed. Your possessions are swept away—or maybe they are looted. You feel vulnerable, helpless, and frightened. In such difficult times, many persons will point angry fingers of blame at the government. But will anger repair the damage? Wouldn't a personal attitude of forgiveness for all shortsighted mistakes made before, during, and after the disaster contribute to an overall social atmosphere of calmness, cooperation, and generosity? Wouldn't a personal attitude of forgiveness help, rather than hinder, the overall task of repairing the damage?

And what if the huge mansion near you was left unscathed by the disaster? What if the millionaire who lives there decides to throw a party, while you are left out in the dark, hungry and cold? What if your rich neighbor does nothing to help you? Would cursing him and wishing for his destruction help to repair the damage to your house? You might hope for freely offered generosity from others, but the frustration of trying to force someone to pay for your damage will only dig you deeper into your own pain.

We might also wonder what could have happened if, in our fictitious story, Mrs. Smith had not been at home when the accident occurred. What if the children had used the broken window as an opportunity to enter into her house and ransack it? What if Mrs. Smith suspected the children but could not prove their guilt?

This raises the issue of cases in which the damage involves not just a material loss but also a personal betrayal. Maybe someone accuses you of untrue things behind your back and it affects your social status. Maybe your business partner steals from you. Maybe a manager fails to uphold a promise. Maybe your husband or your wife commits adultery.

In these cases involving a personal betrayal, keep in mind one important fact:

Forgiveness is not the same thing as forgetting.

To forgive is simply to stop wishing for revenge—that is, to stop wanting to hurt the other person because he has hurt you. But forgiveness is not blind. When trust has been violated you cannot just forget what happened or else the same thing might happen again. There's a saying that unless we remember history we will be condemned to repeat it. So let's face it—even though you might forgive a person who has betrayed your trust, your trust in that person has been crushed.

Trust can be repaired only by time through a gradual process of rebuilding. You have to get to "know" the person all over again. The sad thing is that you may learn that the other person can never be trusted again. On the other hand, if the other person is truly repentant and wants to make a full confession and do penance, the desire to do so will be all that is necessary to nourish a new growth of trust between the two of you.

18 SUGGESTIONS

Truly, it can be hard to forgive anyone if you find yourself dwelling on the dark human desire to "hurt others as you have been hurt." So, instead of focusing on your own thoughts of getting satisfaction, think beyond your own pain. Try thinking about

- the fact that the energy to keep a grudge alive will ultimately drain away your emotional strength and can lead to physical stress-related problems such as gastro-intestinal illnesses;

- the fact that a chronic desire for revenge will ultimately defile your personal integrity and may even unconsciously make you into a person as hurtful and vicious as the person(s) who hurt you;

- the unfortunate life circumstances and

traumas that may have motivated your victimizer;

- the fact that "evil comes to evil" in the end.

No matter what anyone does to you,
no one can take away from you
your capacity to do good.
You lose it only by willingly giving it up yourself.

So remember that if anyone has ever hurt you, you don't
find forgiveness, you *give* it. And if you have ever hurt
others, all you can do is feel sorrow for your behavior;
whether or not others choose to forgive you depends on
them, not on you.

19   A PERSONAL EXPLANATION

"I am having trouble forgiving because my mother is deny-
ing that she abused all of us children and in fact some of my
siblings are choosing to pretend it did not happen and sadly
are repeating the emotional abuse with their own children.
That is where I am at."

Forgiveness is a gift you give to someone else; it's an
act of your own will. And as such your willingness to
forgive your mother does not depend on whether or not
your mother ever acknowledges any of the harm she
caused you.

But even grasping this point intellectually leaves many
persons stymied. "Then what am I supposed to do with
my pain if I can't get any *satisfaction* from the one who
hurt me?" they ask. "How can I get closure?"

Wanting closure is wanting reconciliation, and if the
other person is not willing to repent, then reconcili-

> ation is blocked. Continuing to want closure under
> these conditions is *pride* because it stems from un-
> conscious, unresolved anger on your part to get the
> satisfaction of making the other person repent.

The ultimate answer to your question, therefore, is purely emotional, not logical. Forgiveness comes from your feeling sorrow. Not sorrow for anything that you have done, but sorrow for the very fact that everyone, including yourself, has the same ugly capacity to inflict harm on others, wittingly or unwittingly. Notice the words I just said: *including yourself.* This is where everyone gets stuck, even your siblings, because it is easy enough to see that your mother was hurtful, but to admit that you have the same human capacity for hurt is just too distasteful. In fact, anyone who has been victimized has a human urge to receive compensation, and for you to admit that you and the victimizer are no different from each other—at the human level—is quite terrifying, because it jeopardizes some of that claim to compensation and satisfaction.

Still, it's true that *on the basic human level* you are no different from your mother. She abused you as an unconscious way to get revenge for all the pain inflicted on her as a child, and you refuse to forgive her as a way to get revenge for all the pain inflicted on you as a child. And the fact that your siblings are repeating the abuse only proves the point that they themselves are no different from your mother.

The truth of this, however, does not mean that your pain is not real; nor does it mean that your mother is not responsible for what she did.

But if you can realize that everything she did—although her personal responsibility—was ultimately caused by her own childhood wounds, then you can "see" yourself in her, and in your sorrow you can treat her with mercy.

In forgiving her you ultimately have mercy on yourself, and you free yourself from your greatest burden: hatred. And with that weight lifted, you have the satisfaction of discovering in yourself what you always wanted from your mother anyway: real love.

APPENDICES

APPENDIX I:
A LIST OF EMOTIONS

It has been said, as a joke, that men understand only three emotions: lust, rage, and triumph. Being a man, and having known myself quite well before I began to study psychology, I would say that the joke is not far from the truth.

Anyway, for those who have difficulty identifying their feelings, here is a list of emotions categorized by the most well-known emotions of each group.

Afraid: abandoned, alarmed, anxious, apprehensive, cautious, concerned, desperate, fearful, frightened, hesitant, horrified, hysterical, nervous, panicked, petrified, scared, shocked, threatened, terrified, timid, troubled, worried.

Angry: apathetic, bitter, contemptuous, cross, cruel, defiant, disobedient, enraged, fuming, furious, hateful, heated, hostile, incensed, indignant, infuriated, irate, jealous, livid, mad, mean, outraged, raging, raving, resentful, spiteful, stubborn, unforgiving, vengeful.

Confident: amazed, ambitious, brave, calm, certain, convinced, courageous, determined, empowered, enthusiastic, exhilarated, hopeful, independent, loyal, positive, proud, respectful, secure, strong, triumphant, trusting.

Doubtful: bewildered, bored, cautious, confused, despairing, distant, distrustful, dubious, hesitant, evasive, indecisive, indifferent, insecure, powerless, preoccupied, puzzled, skeptical, suspicious, timid, torn, uncertain, uninformed, wavering.

Happy: calm, carefree, cheerful, comfortable, complacent, contented, ecstatic, elated, enthusiastic, exalted, excited, festive, glad, grateful, inspired, joyous, jubilant, lighthearted, optimistic, peaceful, playful, pleased, relaxed, relieved, satisfied, serene, thrilled.

Hurt: abandoned, crushed, disappointed, disillusioned, disregarded, heartbroken, helpless, misunderstood, offended, rejected, shocked, unnoticed, unwanted.

Interested: absorbed, amazed, ambitious, attracted, awed, concerned, curious, eager, earnest, engrossed, enthusiastic, excited, involved, fascinated, inquisitive, intent, intrigued, sympathetic, pitying.

Irritated: annoyed, exasperated, frustrated, goaded, grumpy, impatient, offended, provoked, shaky, tense, upset.

Loving: accepting, admiring, adoring, affectionate, awed, close, compassionate, considerate, fond, humble, passionate, pitying, sharing, tender, understanding, warm.

Sad: cheerless, defeated, depressed, despairing, dismal, dreary, dull, gloomy, grieving, helpless, hopeless, lonely, low, melancholic, miserable, moody, pessimistic, regretful, remorseful, somber, sorrowful, sulky.

Shamed: disgraced, dishonored, embarrassed, helpless, humiliated, mortified, regretful, remorseful, stupid, ugly, uncomfortable, weak.

APPENDIX II:
DEPRESSION AND SUICIDE

He was about 7 years old. It was after dinner, and the evening sun of midsummer still hung low in the sky. Suddenly, he ran into the house and threw himself onto his bed, crying, saying, over and over through his tears, "I wish I were dead."

As I look back on this event, I can now also recall the rest of the story. My mother had denied me something I wanted (though what it was is long forgotten), I felt unrecognized and unloved, and I was angry at her. In my mind, I began to wish she were dead—but only for a split second, because on the edge of consciousness it occurred to me that if she were to die, I would have no mother. So my mind quickly turned away from that wish for her death, with all of it's lonely implications, and, feeling quite guilty about the whole thing, I began to wish for my own death. After all, what kind of a person could be so dependent on someone else, so helpless and afraid? A no good piece of nothing, that's who, and he deserves to die.

In psychological terms, I had repressed my anger for my mother and ended up turning my frustration against myself. The proverb "Don't bite the hand that feeds you" sums this up nicely. It's a terrible bind for a child. And, if it happens often enough, it can prevent the child from being able to express emotions appropriately—because with every angry thought comes the fear of losing someone's love or protection.

In my own life, beginning with my psychoanalysis as a student, I have had to come to terms with this event and how it has affected my life. I, like many of my own patients, have been forced as an adult to learn how to come to terms honestly with feelings of insult and hurt.

Now, the fleeting suicidal fantasy that I encountered in that moment of childhood frustration was not a clinical case of suicidal depression. Nevertheless, in my professional experience I have seen the dynamic of suppressed anger as a major motive behind clinical depression, and ultimately, as the unconscious motive for serious suicidal thoughts. Someone close to you hurts you, and "Don't bite the hand that feeds you" kicks in from childhood. Fearing the loss of that person's love, you keep silent about your feelings and ultimately—as a way to escape the guilt of your dependency—you be-gin wishing for your own destruction.

But there is one other element to the process.

It isn't just that a person fails to communicate with oth-ers honestly. If you are hurt often enough, in your keep-ing silent about it, and in feeling guilty about being so dependent on someone's love, you can begin to believe not just that you are *unloved* but that you are *despised*. If you ever reach this point, then you seemingly become a "partner" in your own destruction.

> Has anyone ever pushed you away when you want-ed to be held? Has anyone ever given more atten-tion to a bottle of alcohol than to you? Has anyone ever laughed at you when you were hurt? Has any-one ever told you that you were too dumb to suc-ceed? Has anyone ever refused you help when you asked for it? Do you get the idea? No one may have actually told you to kill yourself, but all these sorts of behavioral cues give a clear impression: "You are of no importance to me." "I have no concern for you." "You're not special." "You don't deserve to be alive." "You are garbage."
>
> So, to the "Other," you (and all of us, for that mat-ter) are just an object to be manipulated to satisfy

someone else. It's a losing game to try to make the "Other" love you. It's a losing game to make the "Other" say you're special. Sure, you can try to do all the right things, like drink the right brand of cola, eat at the right fast-food place, wear the right jeans, expose all the right pieces of flesh, pierce and tattoo yourself in the right places, use the right lingo, work for the right company—but once you slip up, then it's the garbage can for you.

Thus you can "tune in" to the resentment of others subliminally, and, if you're not psychologically aware, you can come to believe that these perceptions you receive from others are truth and reality about your personal value—or lack of it.

I'm not trying to tell you here that no one loves you. You can argue all you want that your mother and father love you somehow, and I won't object, because on some level they do love you. The real point is that no human relationships are pure. All the persons in your life who claim to care for you also give indications, through behaviors and things they say and think, that their love is mixed with resentment. It's not pretty to see this directly, so that's why you have defenses that blind you to it. But it's real. At the core, that's where suicidal feelings originate. Not that anyone is necessarily literally wishing you

> to die, but that the feeling of resentment that they
> project can get so strong that you end up feeling
> like garbage. And from there it is only one small
> step to *make yourself* garbage.

Outright child abuse—whether sexual, physical, or emotional—can also contribute to this feeling of being despised. Keep in mind, though, that not everyone who feels, or has felt, depressed or suicidal has been abused as a child. The dynamic of ordinary suppressed anger can be quite sufficient on its own to engender feelings of depression, and, out of a sense of weariness with one's own emotional pain in a callous world, thoughts of suicide can become a seemingly viable option.

Clinical experience and research[8] tell us that child abuse, however, can intensify ordinary existential feelings in several ways.

- *Sexual abuse* essentially amplifies feelings of worthlessness. When an adult sexually abuses a child, the adult is really using the child as an object of pleasure, a mere commodity to be used and then discarded afterwards. Needless to say, being treated like a piece of garbage can leave you believing that you are a piece of garbage. And in feeling that you have lost your humanity, especially if you lack any social support from others, suicide can begin to appear like a fitting conclusion to—and self-inflicted punishment for—a worthless existence.

- *Emotional abuse* essentially amplifies feelings of cynicism, a contemptuous disbelief in human goodness and sincerity. And if you become cynical because you have been belittled so often, not only can you become a bully or a terrorist, but also you can eventually become so weary of the constant fighting against the world and its prejudices that suicide seems like a final revenge.

- *Physical abuse* essentially amplifies feelings of hostility toward—and disrespect for—authority. This simmering animosity can actually harden you to the point that you become cold and calculating in your interactions with others. But if anything ever happens to make you feel that your control of people or events is jeopardized, then, like a soldier in disgrace or a stockbroker gone bankrupt, suicide will seem like your only escape.

So what is the cure for all this dark despair? Well, start

by shattering the illusion that you're a "partner" in your own destruction. Yes, one "part" of your personality may be unconsciously seeking your destruction, but other parts of you do have the authority to listen to and heal this despair.

You feel despised because you despise yourself for hiding your fear and pain.

The irony about depression is that it actually disavows your deepest pain and tries to hide it all with a thick smokescreen of victimization and self-loathing. If you listen to your pain and vulnerability, however, you give yourself the respect and recognition that you can't get from the world, and you take the first step toward your own healing.

Realize, then, that you don't need to destroy your "self," but that you want to put an end to a dependent hiding-behind-your-own-fears way of life while learning how to live honestly and independently in the world.

Suicidal fantasies, when spoken in a therapeutic setting, can actually be quite helpful in getting to some painful emotions that have been suppressed through the years. Of course, it can be difficult and frightening work to voice these feelings—and this points to the fact that it's not life itself that's unbearable—as some desperate persons claim—but it's the thought of facing up to one's own inner pain that *seems* unbearable. Any actual suicide attempt is really a disavowal of love and forgiveness, because in effect you're denying yourself the very things you so desperately desire.

Some people, as a way to "prove" to an uncaring world how despised they feel, and to drown their dishonesty without actually putting an end to it, "gamble" on drugs, alcohol, sex, or even gambling itself to do the job.

But addictions have no payoff except death. The real gamble is with yourself. Will you allow yourself to realize there was nothing wrong with you for wishing your mother or father to be dead? That there was nothing wrong with you for being afraid of your own helplessness? After all, you were just an innocent child in a cruel and frightening world, a world that taught you primarily to fear love.

So who knows what unknown talents you will find in yourself if you face life in a world that is still dangerous, frightening, and cruel?

The world will always be cruel—that's *reality*.

The *illusion* is that the world despises you. The world—

that is, the social world—is simply looking for its own satisfaction; it's not really out to "get you." Even if you were abused as a child—or simply felt neglected—because someone somehow resented you (for example, perhaps you were conceived accidentally, perhaps you weren't the "right" gender, perhaps your siblings were jealous of you for being a new child, or perhaps you were jealous of a new sibling for being a threat to your security) your current mistake is to be deceived by your own pain and end up despising yourself, making self-loathing into a sort of identity.

So remember, to despise yourself is to hide your anger at the world and to run from mercy and forgiveness. If, however, you stop running in fear and learn to live an emotionally honest life, you can then, in mercy, call others into honesty and out of their own illusory social identifications as well. And that's important, because when you reject forgiveness for others, you reject if for yourself, but when you call others to accept accountability for their lives, you discover real love for yourself as well.

NOTES

1. Jacques Lacan, "Aggressivity in psychoanalysis." In *Écrits: A selection*, trans. Alan Sheridan (New York: W. W. Norton, 1977), pp. 8-29.

2. William Shakespeare, *Macbeth, Act V, Scene I.*

3. Maker, A. H., Kemmelmeier, M., & Peterson, C. (2001). Child sexual abuse, peer sexual abuse, and sexual assault in adulthood: A multi-risk model of revictimization. Journal of Traumatic Stress, 14, 351-368.

4. William Shakespeare, *Hamlet*, Act III, Scene IV.

5. St. Teresa of Avila, "The Book of Her Life." In *The Collected Works of St. Teresa of Avila*, Volume Two, trans. K. Kavanaugh and O. Rodriguez (Washington, DC: ICS Publications, 1980). See ch. 32, no. 6:

> [From my vision of hell] "also flow the great impuls-

es to help souls and the extraordinary pain that is caused me by the many that are condemned.

"It seems certain to me that in order to free one alone from such appalling torments I would suffer many deaths very willingly."

6. American Psychiatric Association: *Diagnostic and Statistical Manual of Mental Disorders*, Fourth Edition. Washington, DC: American Psychiatric Association, 1994, Appendix I.

7. Geen R.G., Stonner D., & Shope G.L. (1975) The facilitation of aggression by aggression: evidence against the catharsis hypothesis. Journal of Personality and Social Psychology, 31(4), 721-6.

Mallick, S. K. & McCandless, B. R. (1966). A study of catharsis aggression. Journal of Personality and Social Psychology, 4.

Tavris, C. (1984). Feeling angry? Letting off steam may not help. Nursing Life, 4(5), 59-61.

8. Esposito, C. L., & Clum, G. A. (2002). Social support and problem-solving as moderators of the relationship between childhood abuse and suicidality: Applications to a delinquent population. Journal of Traumatic Stress, 15, 137–146.

ABOUT THE AUTHOR

Raymond Lloyd Richmond, Ph.D. holds his doctorate in clinical psychology and a license as a psychologist (No. PSY 13274) in the state of California.

Previous to his doctoral degree, he earned an M.A. in religious studies and an M.S.E. in counseling.

During the course of his education he received training in Lacanian psychoanalysis, psychodynamic psychotherapy, hypnosis, and cognitive-behavioral therapy. He completed a Post-doctoral Fellowship in Health Psychology at the Department of Veterans Affairs Medical Center in San Francisco.

His clinical experience encompasses crisis intervention; treatment for childhood emotional, physical, and sexual abuse; trauma and PTSD evaluation and treatment; and treatment of psychotic, mood, and anxiety disorders.

He also holds an FAA private pilot certificate.

Dr. Richmond has written and maintains two public-service websites, both of which have no user fees or advertising.

A Guide to Psychology and its Practice
www.GuideToPsychology.com

A secular website
about the practice of clinical psychology.

Chastity – *In San Francisco?*
www.ChastitySF.com

A theological website
about Catholic psychology and
spiritual healing in the Roman Catholic
mystic tradition.

The contents of this book, along with additional information about selected concepts in this book and about the practice of clinical psychology in general, can be found for free on *A Guide to Psychology and its Practice*.

We all know someone who would profit from this book. Keep a few extra copies on hand to share! Consider giving one to your pastor and to those who counsel others. The better they understand these issues, the better they can assist those in their care. Take advantage of our BULK SAVINGS:

1-2 copies	**$7.95 each**	+ $3.00 S/H
3-5 copies	**$6.95 each**	+ $3.50 S/H
6-10 copies	**$5.95 each**	+ $4.50 S/H
11-15 copies	**$4.95 each**	+ $5.50 S/H
16-25 copies	**$3.95 each**	+ $6.50 S/H
26+ copies	**$3.49 each**	+ $7.50 S/H

Please order directly from your bookstore because they need your support. If they don't carry this book, ask them to. But if there isn't a bookstore near you, feel free to order directly from the publisher. Send your order with a check to:

radeMark
PUBLISHING
2223 Wolfangle Road
Cincinnati, Ohio 45244
1-800-433-5504

Or order online at:
www.trademarkstationery.com